How to draw beautiful girls

I0482441

Drawing techniques: Simple tricks that will make you a master

by Amy Hughes

Table of Contents

Disclaimer

While all attempts have been made to verify the information provided in this book, the author does assume any responsibility for errors, omissions, or contrary interpretations of the subject matter contained within. **The information provided in this book is for educational and entertainment purposes only. The reader is responsible for his or her own actions and the author does not accept any responsibilities for any liabilities or damages, real or perceived, resulting from the use of this information.**

The trademarks that are used are without any consent, and the publication of the trademark is without permission or backing by the trademark owner. All trademarks and brands within this book are for clarifying purposes only and are the owned by the owners themselves, not affiliated with this document.

Introduction

Have you been looking for a way to improve your drawing techniques? Have you been trying to find a hobby that doesn't require loads of effort in exercising? Or better yet, you need to express a message to a large crowd but you find it hard to spend time and resources in translations and printing massive copies that carry the same message? Well, you have found what you have been searching for, this book has been written to suit all your needs, containing the most modern methods, your drawing career is bound to kick off with a unique dimension, experience how simple and effortless it can be to draw what you once saw as a complex professional drawing, have fun as you work on your drawings and most importantly gain interest in drawing.

Over a decade and a half, I have worked as an artist in my small workshop in my garage; I have also managed to teach hundreds of students and passed on first hand experiences and knowledge to most of the artists who have grown to be well re-known all over the globe. I began drawing when I was in my early twenties, my passion to draw grew differently from the rest; I consider it as an inspiration. During one of my expeditions abroad I passed by a poor neighborhood in Asia and got to experience some harsh conditions that the dwellers experienced daily, I was then determined to help out and show the world of what goes on in such areas without words, I wanted everyone to actually grasp the feeling that I had and feel how it was like then make a difference by helping out. After months of recording videos and spending lavishly on editing and publishing, I released the final video to the world but it dint get much attention as I expected, in short it turned out to be a complete loss.

Showcasing and communicating to the world of this poor neighbourhood was my number one agenda but day after day it turned out to be harder than I thought, I was running out of finances and had to look for a new way to make my voice heard without spending as much as I spent on making videos. That was when I was invited to one of the local drawing exhibits where I got to see a little girl's painting stand out and speak to a large crowd, in an instant the thought of drawing struck my mind, it dint take the young girl a lot of resources to make her drawing, it was only some pencils and some charcoal, nothing pricy or complicated and People were able to blend with it and get hear the young girl's voice, so I set out to make my own drawing and within three months it was ready, it wasn't easy at first but the drive that I carried deep within me led me to finish it. The drawing reached out to a larger number than I ever thought, the video wasn't impactful as it was, plus people could easily interpret. Now that's the power of drawing, you can use it as a great communication tool.

Drawing is the new form of communication, more people are embracing and loving it each day, compared to traditional hard techniques, the modern form of drawing has been made significantly simple thanks to a number of numerous developments and improvements in technology. Over five in every ten people globally have taken drawing as a hobby, by reading this book; you will be getting to learn some of these techniques, you will discover a new power within you, everybody has a unique aspect to offer, you will always have something unique in drawing.

Did you know that drawing sharpens your thoughts and awakes your nerves? I t has been proved that artists generate a sense of calmness and ease while drawing, this in turn relaxes the body and enhances circulation flow throughout the body, enhanced circulation flow will ease your mind and awaken your senses. This book contains steps that will calm you and help fin relaxation of your body.

Besides that, there are other medical benefits of drawing such as in recovery and also mind development. Drawing is essential for everyone; by learning the different drawing skills you will not only be making some cash but also be meditating and developing your personality.

Drawing has been there since history, you have probably seen some ancient drawings on caves or mountains, these drawings were meant to communicate and beautify, you also can communicate and beautify, this book has the techniques to elevate your drawing, you will be making history in a fun enjoyable way, hold on and see the difference, Have fun as you draw the lady!

First Technique

Drawing tools

These are simply all the apparatus you will need to kick start your drawing ventures, it might seem as not such a big deal but the kind of tools you use will determine the quality and appearance of your drawing. Think of your apparatus as building materials, if you build a house from stone, it will be stronger and long lasting than of wood or mud, same applies to drawing, from the pencils, erasers, drawing surfaces and much more.

The good thing about this book is everything is detailed; you will save a lot of time and resources in finding scarce information. It's not in every place that you will find everything in order.

An artist can be good enough but his or her tools can make them rookies in their field, hence the importance of choosing not only drawing material but quality applicable material.

Have a look at this drawing below, observe it carefully,

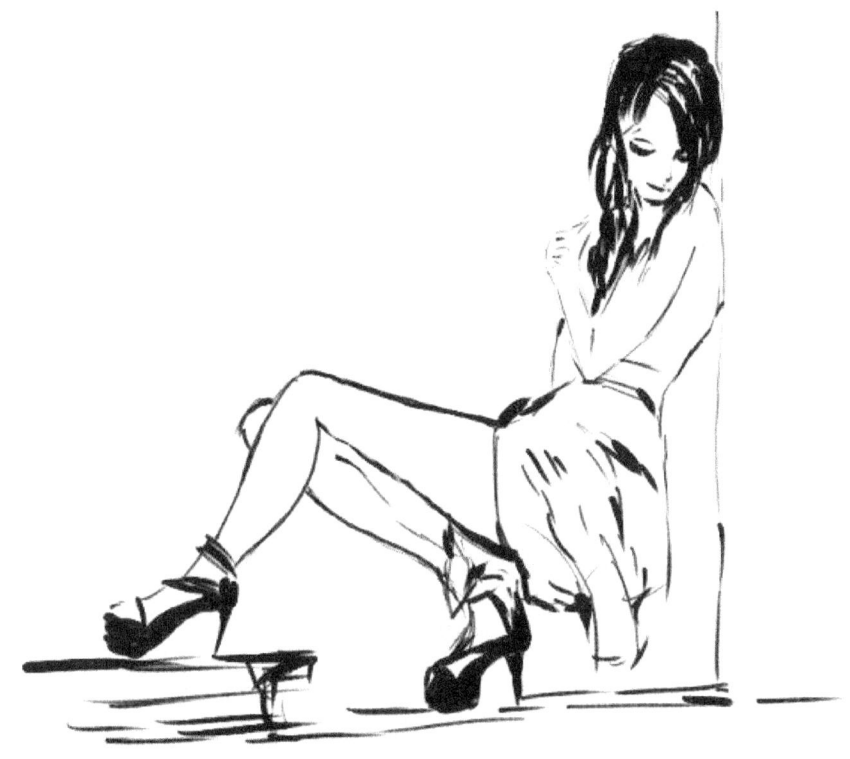

According to you, how long do you think the artist took t such and what were the tools he used? As

Why it's important to choose the right drawing materials

1. To maintain Quality

Quality is what makes your drawings unique and standing out, with the right tools, your drawing will not be below standards despite the outcome; we are living in an age where people prefer quality than quantity. If you plan to make a drawing that will reach out to a larger audience, invest in quality materials.

2. To avoid unnecessary improvisations

Each and every one of us who attended the lower classes has at one point improvised either their writing or drawing tools, whether it was that elastic band you used as an eraser or that pencil you chewed off, broke off or bit to reach to the black graphite due to lack of a sharpener. You know how improvisations can mess up your work, when you sharpen a blunt pencil in the middle of a drawing, you are bound to change the entire style of the rest of the drawing; the same applies to erasing. To avoid these unnecessary and unplanned for changes, you can find a set of quality tools that will prevent that from happening.

3. To be above standards and professionalism

A professional artist is made by using the right tools, there is simply no short cut in this, and professionalism means the ability to provide nothing but the best, your drawing will fail to grasp the viewers' attention if it's below standards, it will only steal their attention if it stands out. To make your drawing stand out, use quality material that is bound to sparkle your drawing and leave no stains or dirt.

4. To make work easier

The right tools are there to make work easier, consider carrying a heavy load with your hands and carrying it with a carrier for example a wheelbarrow, it would be much easier and safe to carry it with a carrier instead of your own hands whereby you might just drop it when you can't hold on anymore. The same applies to drawing; the wrong tools are not predictive plus are time consuming since you spend much time in repeating. Your drawing can either turn out to be good or bad whereas on the other hand, the right tools save you time and energy.

5. To get things in order

When things are in order, the better they work and make work easier, a simple example would be a machine, any machine or computer whatsoever, the gadgets inside these machines work in order to give better services, if they are not in order, the quality of the service provided declines. The same is directly proportional to drawing, the moment you stop drawing because you have to look for that pencil or other item you need in your drawing, what you would have done will be completely different since you will lose focus on your drawing and focus more on finding the tool. If you can manage to be organized, your work will improve in quality as you won't lose your focus.

Those are just some of the main benefits of drawing; there are plenty you will find along as you proceed to the next chapters. Have a look at the following image, it might seem simple but its attention grasping since the artist used the right materials.

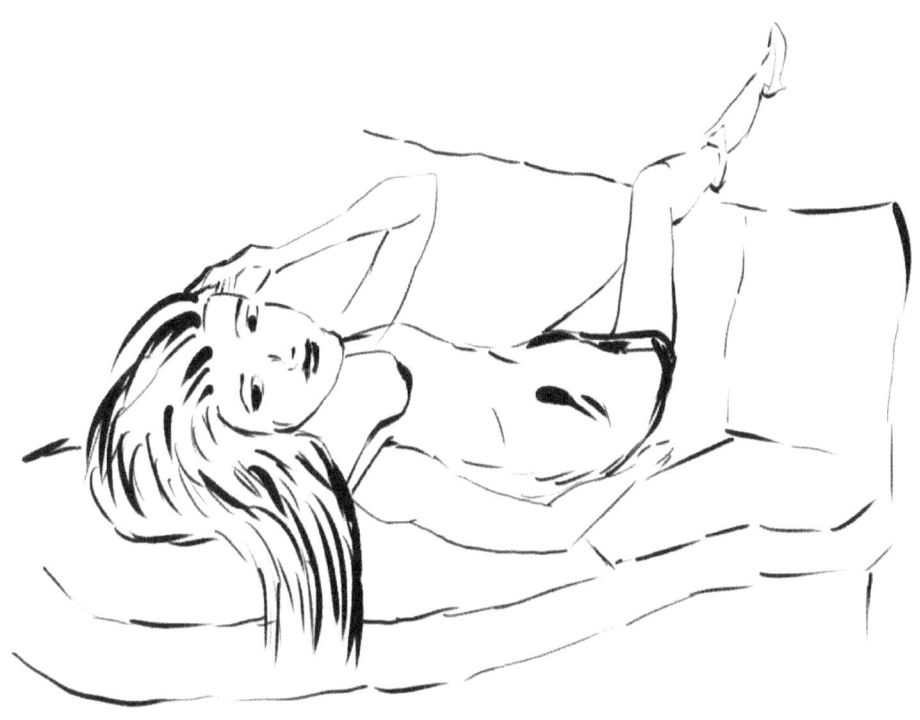

The drawing tools

1. The pencils

The pencil is second main tool. It is what you relate with as an artist, a pencil you will blend with might take time to find but the faster you find it, the quicker your strides will be. Pencils either come in sets or in singles, as you begin your drawing ventures it would be wise to purchase a set rather than singles, this is because the set usually comes with a variety of different pencils arranged according to grade. This grade is the thickness or thinness of the graphite inside, the graphite is the black part of the pencil.

A set of pencils will be much appropriate for a beginner since beginners usually don't have much know-how of the different grades of pencils. However, if it's a pro, singles would be better as you already know which type and make will best fit.

2. Drawing surface

The drawing surface is where you will transfer your drawing from the sketch book; it is where you present your imagination, portrait or vision. It should therefore be big enough so as to make the perfect sketch that your audience can easily interpret.

A good drawing surface can be identified by taking the following into consideration:

I.   The texture of the paper

Also commonly referred to as the tooth is the compactness and texture of the surface; some surfaces are hard while others are easy. The texture of the surface is a determinant to the outcome of your drawing. A hard surface can be tormenting to a new beginning artist but can also be a joyride for the experienced artist. A hard surface will make the drawing bumpy as the pencil might not glide properly. A smooth surface on the other hand is the beginning artist's joy, it doesn't require a technique like in the hard surface where you have to keep your hand still throughout the bumps. The final drawing on a smooth surface seems flawless and rigid in many occasions.

II.   The weight of the paper

The weight of the paper is the total ream that is carried by that paper, different surfaces have different reams they can be heavy and others can be light, for beginners, it would be wise to choose a surface with a light rim, it is easily foldable but requires less pencil skills than in the heavier one.

III.   Reaction of the paper to acidity

You probably have come across an old book and became surprised as to how some pages seem yellow while others aren't, well this is because different pages have different levels of acidity freedom. The page that is white is said to be acid resistant; that is its rate of tolerance to UV light and any other form of acidity in the atmosphere is higher than the yellow page. A yellow page simply means that the paper isn't acid resistant and will not last long. When choosing a drawing surface, chose the surface that has high resistance.

Here are some kinds of papers or surfaces that you can experiment with to gain further understanding on the tooth and the ream;

a. Bristol paper- has a smooth texture and heavier ream

b. Charcoal surface paper – heavier in ream and smooth in texture, also seems transparent

c. Common drawing paper – Is medium in texture between rough and smooth and also average in weight.

3. Sketchbook

The sketchbook is the rough drawing or where the artist collects his drawing samples before transferring them to his or her drawing surface, it therefore should be big enough for the artist to make lots of drawings, big in the number of pages but not the surface area, an average sized sketch book would do just fine since its portable and not that heavy to carry around.

The sketchbook should be something that you are comfortable with, it should be something that you can place on your lap and draw effectively without struggling, it should be a good size for you, a size that you can fit in your bag or pocket. The sketch book is something that an artist should always carry along, whenever you get a glimpse of something you want to draw, all you do is take it out and make a quick drawing that you later transfer to your drawing surface.

4. Erasers

Erasers are there to clear off mistakes, and there are a variety to choose from, every artist makes mistakes, it's part of human nature; therefore don't be too hard on yourself. Here are the different forms of erasers:

i.   Rubber eraser

The rubber eraser is the most common form of eraser, used to remove graphite from pencils on paper. This form uses friction to erase.

ii.   Kneaded rubber

The kneaded rubber is used when lifting materials off the drawing surface, unlike the rubber eraser that uses friction, the kneaded rubber sticks to the surface and erases by pulling up, it is flexible and can stretch into any size or shape, it gets dirty quickly but is cleaned by kneading.

iii. The crumble

Also referred to as the gum eraser, is a special kind of eraser that erases by sticking onto the material then with friction erases while crumbling on the drawing surface, it is used in scenarios where the drawing surface is delicate and could tear.

5. Sharpeners

Sharpeners come in different varieties; there are electrical and manual types. When it comes to these sharpeners, there are some that are good while others are not that good, a good sharpener takes less time to sharpen and does it without wasting much of the pencil while a bad sharpener takes lots of time in sharpening, wastes a lot of the pencil and doesn't sharpen accordingly, it is therefore important to consult the shop attendant on the different qualities of the sharpener.

6. Drawing/art storage

This is where you will be storing your drawings. A drawing surface needs to be a clean and conducive environment for your drawing. It also needs to be secure and free from public viewing, as described in the introduction; everybody has a unique way of expressing themselves in art form, the art form that you come up with will be different from the rest and it just might be worth more than you think, now Imagine if someone got to see what you were drawing then went off and made a similar drawing, you would have lost a lot. To choose the right art storage, consider the following:

i.   Size of the storage tool

The bigger the size the better, this is because you might probably need much space in the future when you are now good enough to make big drawings. A hollow large pipe can be good; you can improvise it in such a way that you can roll your drawings and place them inside then find a lead.

ii. Rigidness of the storage tool

The rigidness of the art storage item is the strength and compactness to with stand pressure and safe guard your drawings, a hard covered storage material will protect your drawings from damage by folding while a water proof material will safe guard your drawings from humidity and any form of liquid or water.

iii. Portability

Have a form of artwork storage that can both be used for safety of your drawings and also portable, you might be requested to carry along some of your drawings in exhibitions or for some one prominent to have a look at.

Also the storage should be humidity proof, by this I mean that you should store your drawings inside where moisture and other forms of acidity and pollution will not affect it, remember the acidity freedom factor as mentioned in the earlier stages of this step.

7. Charcoal

Each day artists are moving into charcoal drawing, charcoal drawing involves drawing with pieces of charcoal. Most artists proclaim that they are able to draw faster when they use charcoal, plus the sketching is made much easier.

Second technique

The image

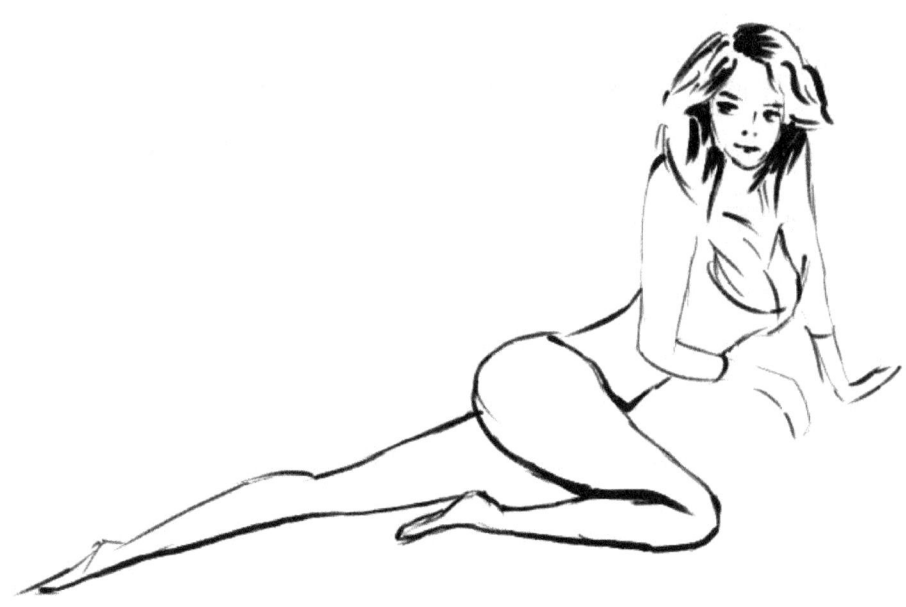

The image is what inspires you to do the drawing, it might be something or somebody you admire, love or is close to. The image you choose will determine how long your drawing venture will be, it is therefore important to not only choose but to choose the right.

Choosing the right image can be mentally and physically draining, you can spend lots of hours trying to figure out what is not too hard or too simple to draw and in the end become less motivated to venture into the wonderful amazing world of drawing, a lot of people often quit because of failing to choose the right image as they begin doubting their abilities along the way but you don't have to worry, you won't be quitting anything here, I got your back on this, choosing an image has never been made easier, I understand that you want something simple and fancy, something that you won't quit halfway but will get done with it and move on to the next, something that will bring out that amazement and applaud by your viewers, well this is how you get to do it best, by knowing exactly which steps to take when choosing.

As you can see from the lovely sexy girl image above, the drawing doesn't have to be complex to stand out, what really matters is how you bring your idea into paper and the life it has with the ability to grasp the attention of the viewer.

Here are a few factors to take into consideration when choosing the right image:

1. **Outline of the image**

The outline of the image is the shape of the image or model you want to draw, some objects and models are easy to draw if they have an upright and uncomplicated posture. However, it might be tough for the beginner to draw some postures, as they are not conversant and experienced with the techniques of shaping some complicated edges and corners. As a beginner, try out some simple Images, they simple images you practice on will strengthen you to draw the complex images that you have always wanted. Drawing is more like a sport; you start with the easy stuff before peaking to the tough challenging stuff. Below are some images that I will show you how to draw in the fourth coming steps. They are good for you to start with.

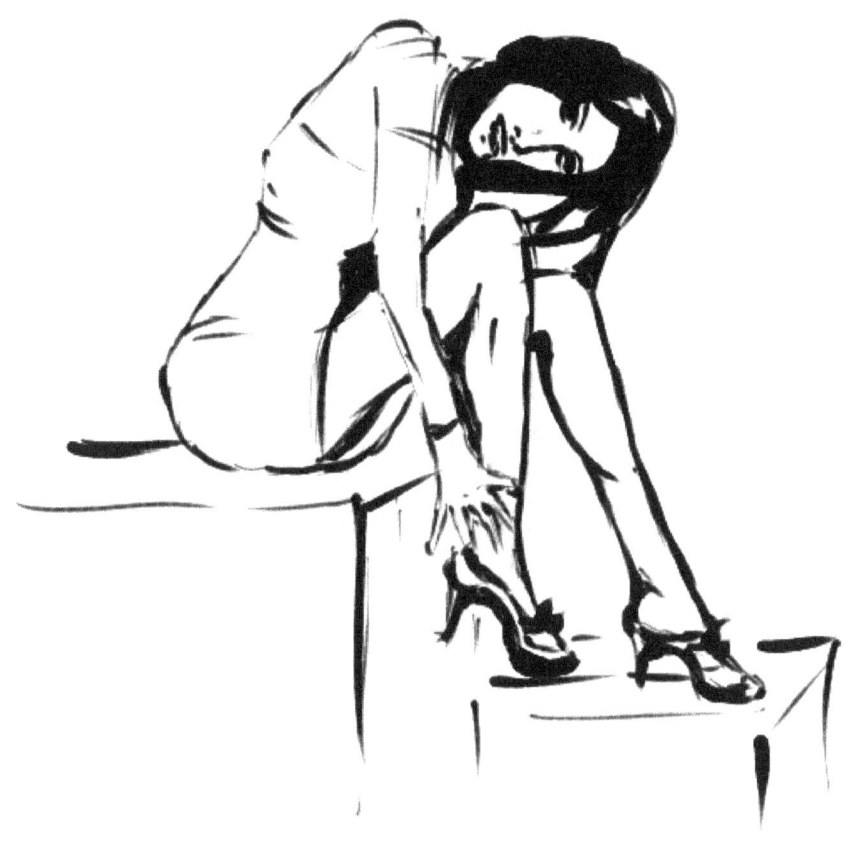

As you can see from the diagram of the girl above; the drawing is not that complicated, it's simple, as you read on the next chapters, you will get to learn more about new styles and how to go about it, its unbelievably easy, you can also choose from this other one below:

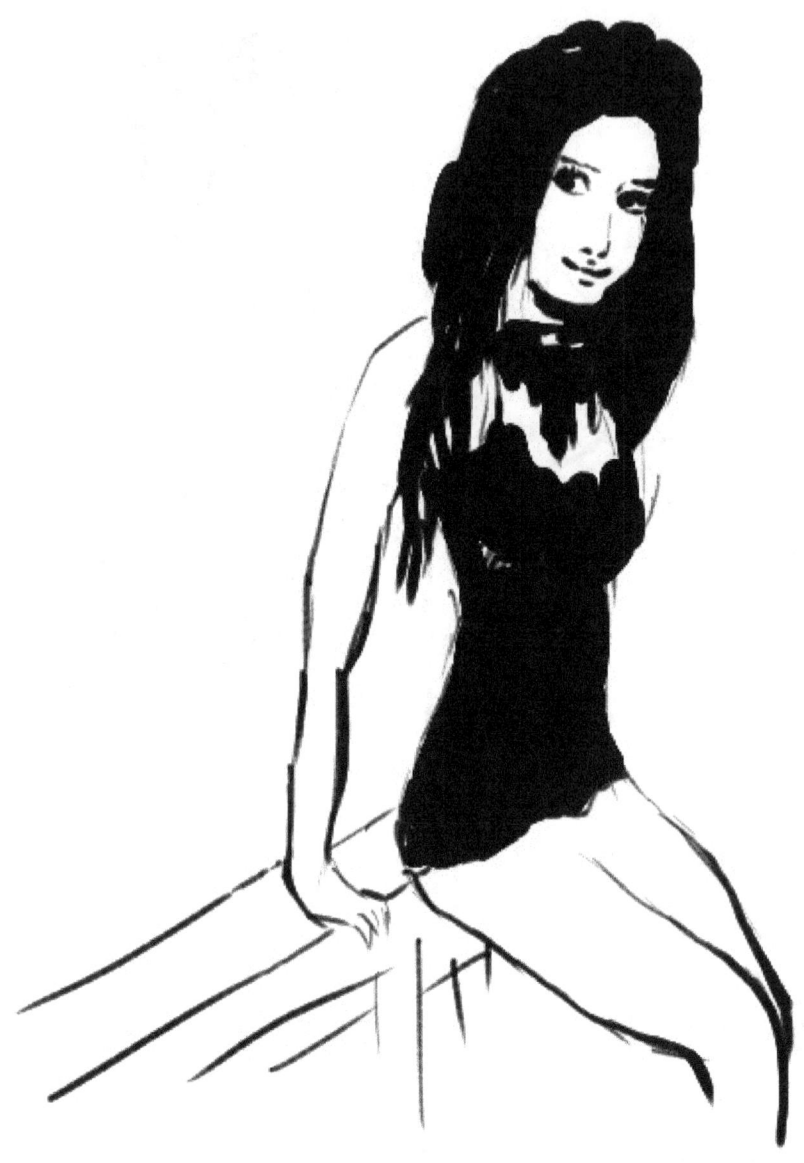

Now that is an image you can get done within twenty minutes max, challenge yourself, notice the thick shading inside the outline, also take note of the corners, there is a style for that too.

2. Anatomy of the image

The anatomy of the image is the life of the image, it is the life you put in your drawing, for example look at this photo;

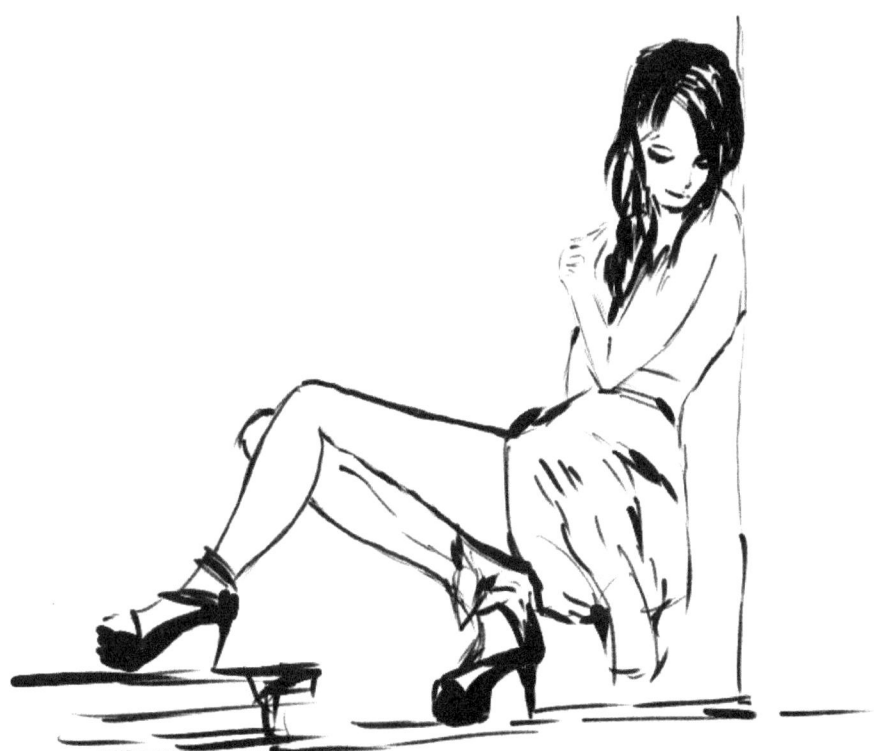

Notice how the girl's eyes are closed as she stares to the floor while her skirt falls out under her thighs, the fact that you are able to see the skirt falling off is anatomy, the fact that the girl is staring down with eyes closed, expresses that she is worried or in deep sadness, now that's bringing out life in the drawing. Try another image out, use anatomy to bring the reality into the drawing.

3. Current drawing level

When choosing an image, take into consideration your experience, don't choose something complex such as a 3D drawing or the Mona Lisa, I understand that you are challenging your potential but remember all great drawings were not made within an hour or a day, they took time and lots of concentration to be what they are. Start off with the easy ones first, they will save you a lot from quitting; reflect on this, to begin driving on the main road you need a license, and to get that license you must have practised.

4. Motivation

Motivation is the drive within you, it is what you look up to when your drawings seems to go nowhere, choosing an image that you will associate with is recommended, what you are attached to or admire will strengthen you to keep going, a lot of people usually quit halfway because of lack of inspiration, make sure that what you choose is something you can work with and can hold you up when you are losing interest. You can also find motivation by visiting museums and other art sceneries, there you will find all sorts of drawings and be amazed by some fabulous unique drawings and paintings you will learn a few things from there.

5. Think outside the box

Don't confine your mind to only think of what it sees or hears, go beyond your mind horizons by trying out new stuff like drawing your shoe or somebody who is idle at home watching TV, the opportunities are endless, I once drew a drunken old man sleeping on the bench and sold it for a good price. Don't limit yourself.

Practice

Relax, your mind while seating or lying down somewhere comfortable, close your eyes and imagine someone or something that means a lot to you, freeze their image on your mind and study their outline and anatomy, minimize the image and make it black and white, study the image, their outline, how they are posed and let the image freeze on your mind.

Open your eyes and take out your sketch book, draw the image you have on your mind beginning with the outline, close your eyes when you seem to get lost and check the image on your mind again, keep drawing till you are done, now look at your sketchbook, it might be perfect or have a few errors, that was your first imaginary drawing and you just gained a unique ability on drawing.

Third step

The pencil drawing techniques

After learning about the different types of apparatus used in drawing and how to get the right image to draw from the previous steps, you are now a step away from becoming a professional artist, the only thing left for you to do is get to know the different techniques and how they are applied plus some extensive drawing. All those side cartoons on your books or papers are actually potential, the doodles that you also make are also valuable, as you recall from the earlier step of the book; everyone has a unique artistic side that they can showcase to the world. It's always fun to draw.

There are several drawing techniques involved, these are simply the many methods that are used to make drawing easier and classy; a good blend of techniques on an image brings out a high quality dazzling drawing. You probably have heard of these drawing techniques and ignored them at some point, might be because you thought they are complex or better yet you simply have no interest or in most cases don't know what they are, well, don't panic, we have everything detailed for you, here are some of the main reasons as to why you should get to know these techniques:

Importance of pencil techniques

1. Save time

By utilising these techniques, you save a lot of time in making amendments and adding some parts to the drawing, it is also time saving since as you sketch quickly especially when the image is moving.

2. Make work easier

Pencil techniques were actually formed as a way to end the difficult boring task of drawing then erasing till the artist gets the right shape or shade.

3. Add the quality of your drawing

Pencil techniques are guaranteed to leave your drawing with a professional quality touch, they are the blueprint to the drawing standards; it's very easy to differentiate a normal drawing from a professional drawing thanks to this techniques, use them as they have lots of advantages.

4. Are easy to use and require no special ability

Pencil techniques are the simplest and require zero special abilities; everyone can draw them as long as they can hold their pencil. It's just a matter of playing with your pencil and getting the most out of it.

5. Bring out the life of your drawing

Using different pencil techniques in a drawing is the only way you can ever bring life to your drawing, try it without and your drawing will look as if you sketched a whole bunch of errors. Always try out pencil techniques, they never let down.

6. Are used in bringing out the 2D effect in drawings

Simple pencil techniques can change the entire outlook of your drawing, I once drew my hand then used the shading pencil technique; the final drawing was different and great it carried that two dimension outlook and you could tell where the source of light was coming from.

The outline form of pencil technique

The first pencil technique is the outline creation; it involves drawing the shape of the image before drawing the rest of the inner parts inside the outline: Here are some diagrams to explain further:

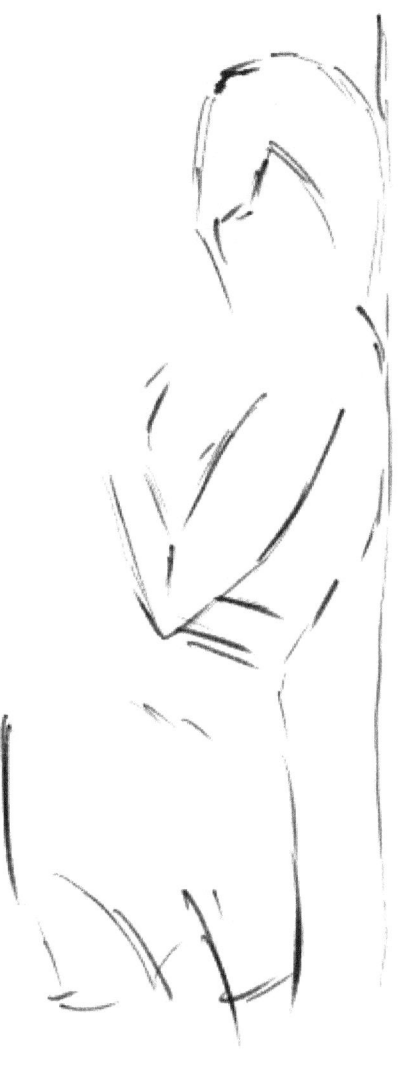

Above is the outline of the photo of the girl seated to the ground, here the outline is the only technique that has been utilised. Take a look at these others:

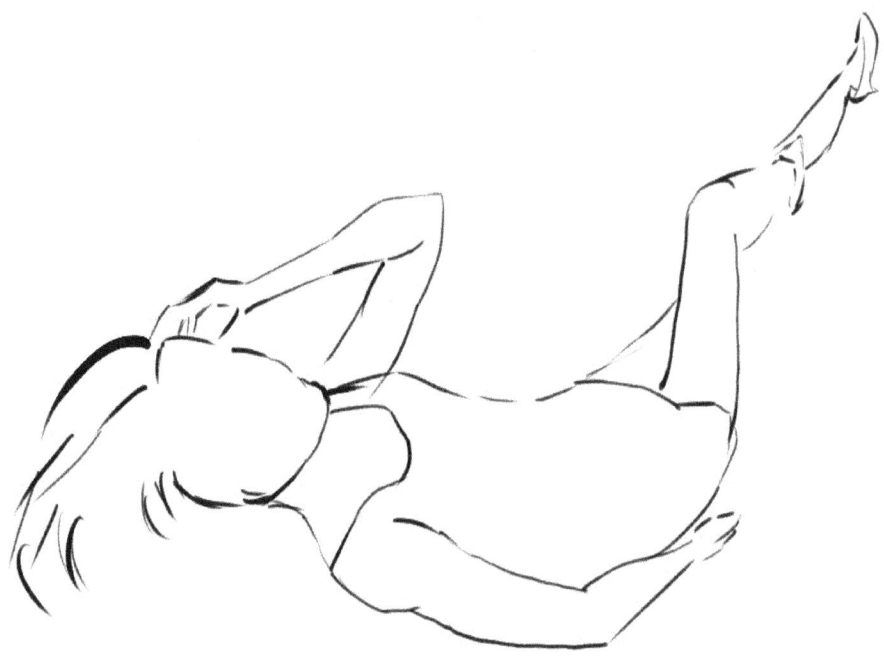

Above is the outline shape of the girl lying upside down her couch, you will notice that the artist has only used thick lines to shape out the outline, but in the real sense before making the thick lines, the artist first of all uses a sharp low-grade pencil to shape out, he or she then covers the faint stripes by exchanging his low-grade pencil with a high-grade blunt pencil and passes it over the faint stripes forming thick layers.

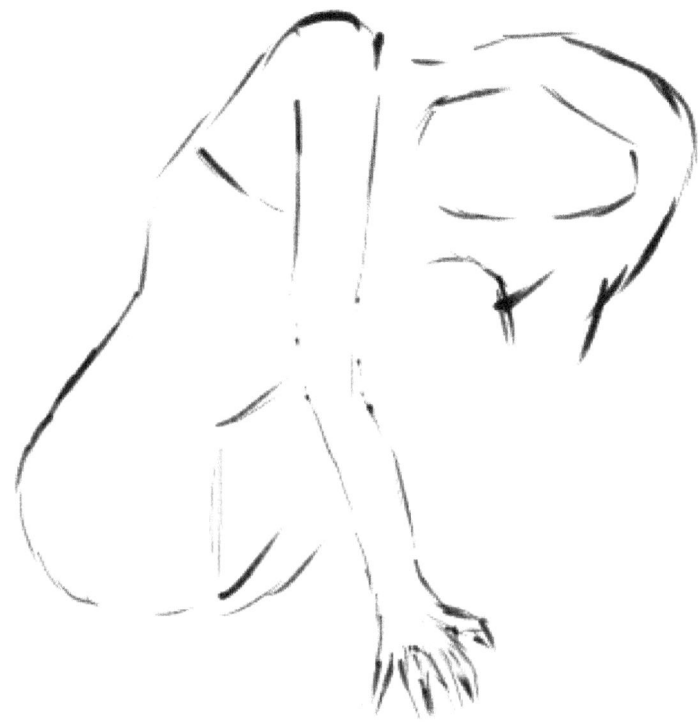

Look or magnify closely and you will see the faint marks.

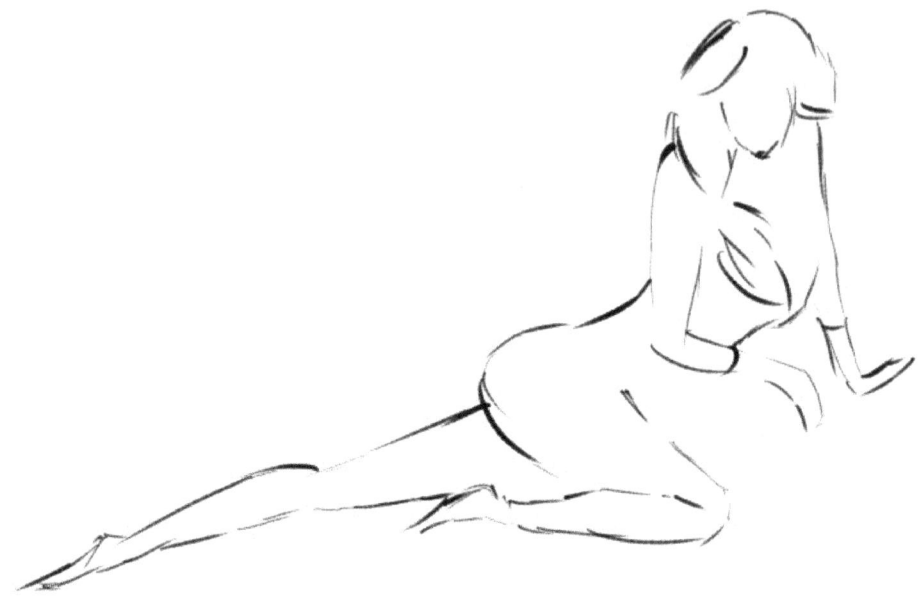

After drawing the outline, we now come to the next step which involves drawing the interior of the outline, the interior of the outline is where the real essence of the drawing is felt.

Practice

During your free time look for some objects to draw and place them on the table, or anywhere where you have a good view, they don't have to be all necessarily objects but also some photos from magazines and newspapers, then draw their outlines at first without timing yourself.

After you have done that, now draw those objects and images while timing yourself give yourself around twenty minutes for each, this will help outstandingly in increasing your drawing speed and the way you look at things.

2. Hatching

Hatching is the second form of pencil technique, it is whereby an artist draws faint or thick lines overlying on top of each other on the outline or inside the outline to give the image a more realistic look.

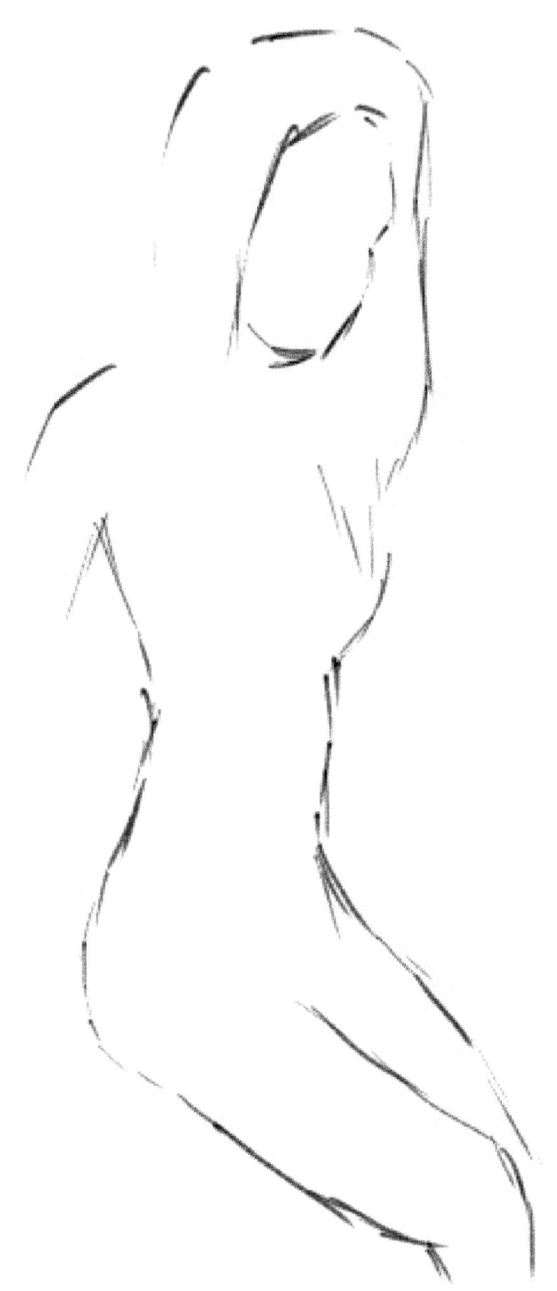

As you can see from the image above there are faint lines covered by thick lines overlying on top of each other, that is hatching, if the outline was made to consist of a long unending line the real essence in the drawing wouldn't be noticeable, it would be a direct drawing, not carrying any 2D effects.

Apart from Hatching only, there is also the cross hatching technique, the cross hatching technique occurs when lines that are arranged in the same direction close together, are crossed by lines from the opposite direction in order to make the drawing real and attractive.

Practice

Draw a soccer ball outline then hatch it outline, do you notice any change? Now draw some cross hatches inside the alignment of the ball, what do you notice? You should have noted that the image has changed to a two dimension image and the reality essence has been maximised.

3. Circular techniques

Circular techniques comprise of drawing faint circular lines over the image to create a texture feeling within the image, for example if I draw two trees together and some bushes growing between them and I have the intention of creating a desert feature on the drawing, I will make circular scribbles at the base of the trees to bring out the roughness of the surface.

To make these circular techniques, swirl your faint pencil in circles closely together avoiding the going over halfway the tree's stem, now look at the photo, the first impression you might get would be there is wind blowing between the trees or there is dust all over, just like a real desert.

Circular techniques are basically used for bringing out the texture of the drawing, always make sure that you use a low grade pencil when circling your photos, choose as 6B when circling and make sure the pencil is sharp but not in a way that it could tear off the whole drawing surface.

Practice

Draw an abandoned street where there is litter lying everywhere and the leaves are being swept away by the wind, you can add a tree on the far corner, now using the hatching, cross hatching and circular techniques make the drawing stand out and be a two dimension. Make sure that your viewers will easily interpret the circles as a rough texture caused by the dust on the air.

4. Shading

There are different kinds of shading with the main examples being hatching and cross hatching, apart from that you can also paint or colour with a felt tip pen of any colour you like i.e., if your drawing is too basic, you can also shade by using charcoal, charcoal shades a larger area fast. Below are images of the lady in different poses after shading.

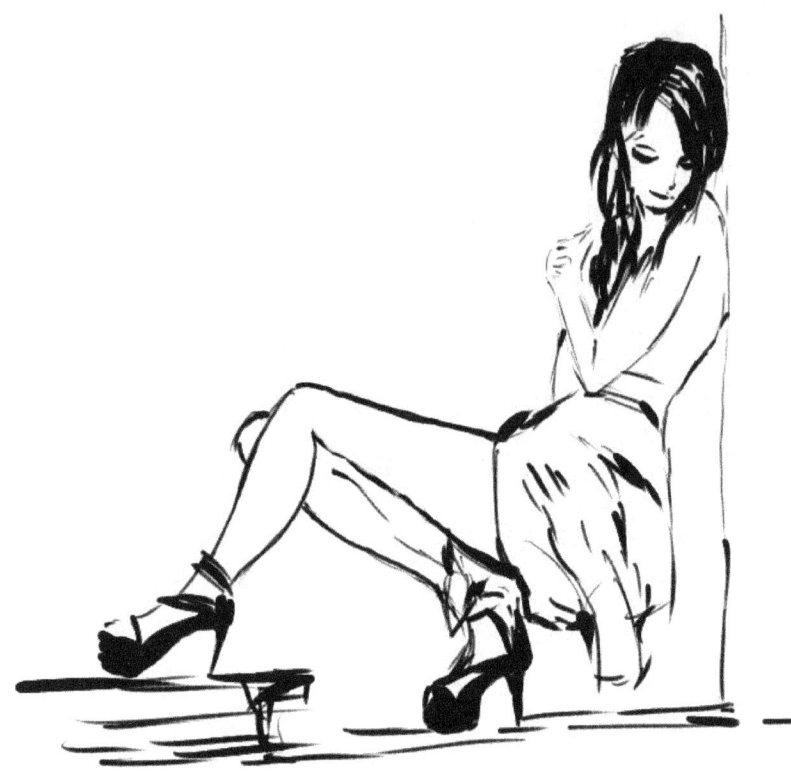

Notice how the hair and the shoes are shaded, the artist used a
thick pen to do this, in this case this form of shading is the
hatching methods as it incorporates lines drawn close together
heading the same direction.

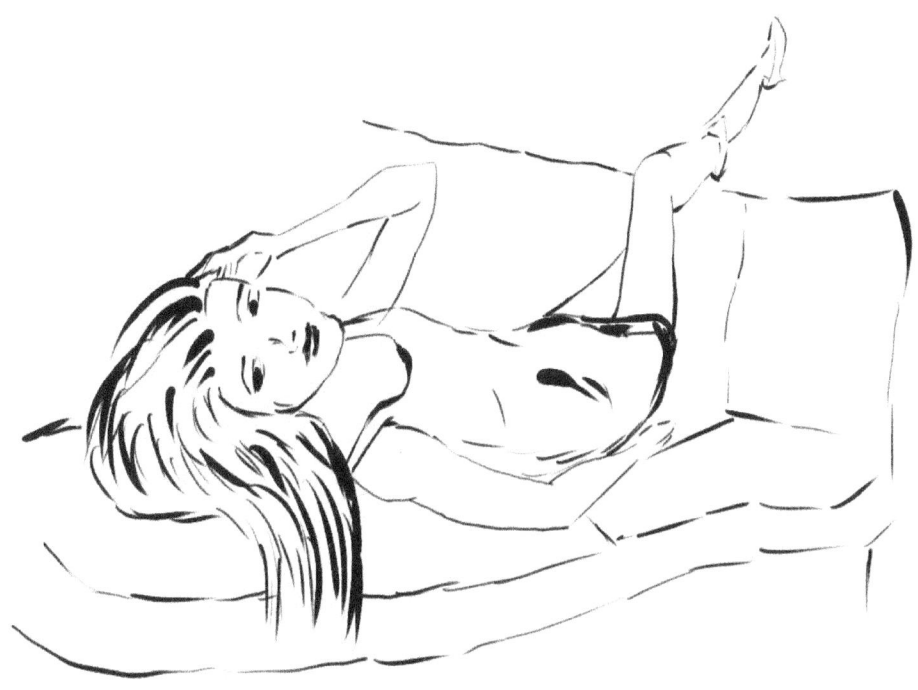

On this photo the artist has used different types of marked pens to shade, there is the thin pen and the thick pen, by using a mixture of both on the hair, the reality essence of the drawing is experienced, it seems better than shaded completely.

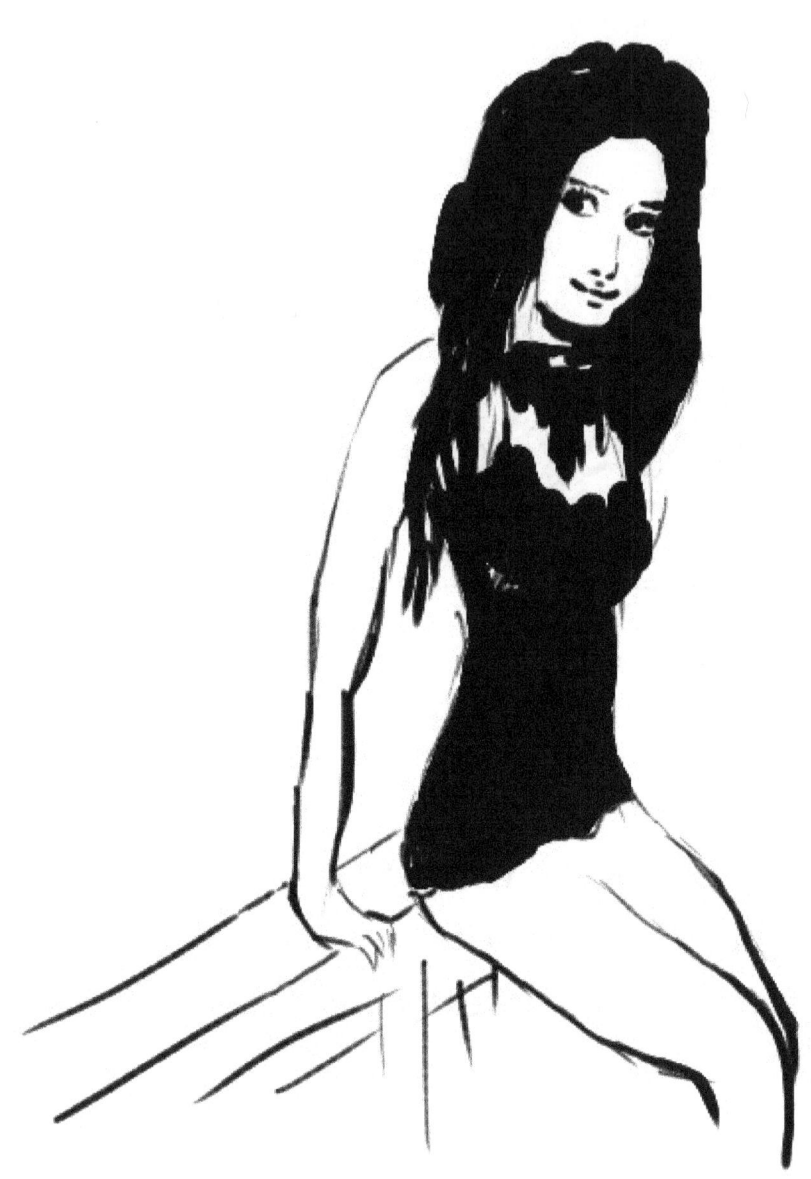

The photo above has a lot you can dig about, there is the outline that has been overlaid with the continuous black marker and also the dark hair and the top the girl is wearing, here the artist seemed to have used only one type of marker, he or she seems to be experienced as any slight usage of that marker again would have ruined the whole drawing, be cautious while shading such, it might lead to a repeat of the whole drawing.

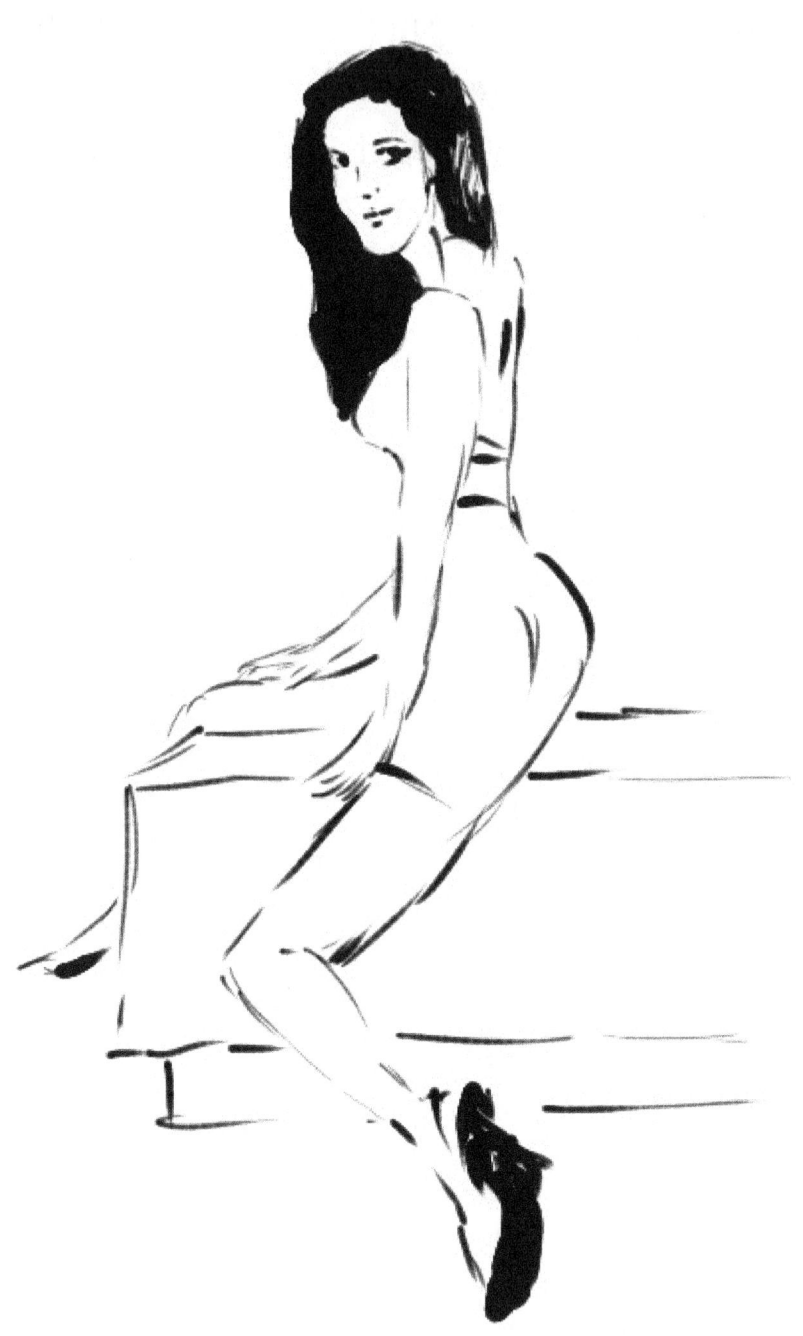

From this image the artist really tried as it seems as if they were in a hurry, the overlapping hatching technique saved the artist from most of the parts such as the hands and right leg.

You will also notice also that the quality of the image was greatly altered by the choice of the tools the artist chose. Whenever you are drawing, make sure that all the apparatus are standby, as said earlier, the right tools for the best quality.

Keep practising on this and many more images, the more you practice the better, the more you will gain more experience and become a true professional. I wish you all the best!

Conclusion

Thank-you for purchasing this book, I hope that it has been of much help to you as it was for me while writing, you can now comfortably draw any image you ever wished, drawing is the new black as they say, it has many benefits both health wise and career wise, despite the many ages it has been in existence, it still remains one of the untapped and half utilised areas with potential to make the world into a better place.

Drawing has no specific date of discovery; it was there since time, the early man used to draw as means of beautifying his cave as well as to educate the young ones, it was there even before man made language. Ever since, the world of drawing has developed with time, compared to the historical times, only the skilled would draw, it would take a lot of time and effort to be an artist as the resources were minimal and the teachers were few, to get something to draw with was tough as technology was not that advanced like in our times where we can even draw on tablets or phones and there are lots of drawing materials. However, old is gold, some of the historical paintings have remained intact even after the test of time; they have surpassed the acidity test compared to the modern forms of drawing surfaces.

Drawing has since been made public after the revolution period, people are still embracing it and practising it all over the globe, drawing has remained the only activity that has never been affected after centuries of transformation, it also remains the best in offering jobs but many are still reluctant to take it as a career. However, despite the robust staunch drawing has stood, modern trends are accusing it as a tool used to criticize and insight negatively, people have begun hiding coded messages in drawings that carry secrets that could change the world, this trend has proved to be unstoppable and of major concern to security services globally, there has been a huge number of upcoming cults due to this which has led to talks and debates among international leaders that drawings should be scanned before presenting to the public to avoid such.

Despite the negative reviews on drawing, it still is a developing industry, many are turning into it to make a livelihood and raise their families especially in the third world countries. Drawing is an industry that was there before time and continues to fascinate and baffle the best of scholars; many claim it's a source of coded information but still it stands strong and remains as the untapped industry that has the ability to re-revolutionize the world more than any other.

I hope you have gained a lot about drawing and what it entails, before you leave check out my other books that are exciting and informative, I wish you the best as you kick off your drawing ventures, remember everyone has a unique feature that the world is waiting to experience.

www.ingramcontent.com/pod-product-compliance
Lightning Source LLC
Chambersburg PA
CBHW080551190526
45169CB00007B/2729

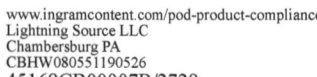